THE RIGHT PROSPECTUS

The Right Prospectus

a play for television

by

JOHN OSBORNE

FABER AND FABER
London

First published in 1970
by Faber and Faber Limited
24 Russell Square London WC1
Printed in Great Britain by
Latimer Trend & Co Limited Plymouth
All rights reserved

ISBN 0 571 09478 1 (paper edition)
ISBN 0 571 09479 1 (cloth edition)

All professional inquiries in regard to this play should be addressed to the author's agent, Margery Vosper Ltd, 53a Shaftesbury Avenue, London W1, and all amateur inquiries should be addressed to Messrs. Evans Brothers Ltd, Montague House, Russell Square, London WC1.

Cast

YOUNG BOY

GROUPS OF BOYS

BOYS ON CRICKET PITCH

HEAD

JENKINS

NEWBOLD

MRS. NEWBOLD

FIRST DRIVER

SECOND DRIVER

FIRST BOY

MR. TESTER

GROOM

SHIPPARD

SECOND BOY

THIRD BOY

TINY

HEFFER

STAFF

SENIOR BOY

JUNIOR BOY

PARTRIDGE

MATHS MASTER

MASTER ONE

MASTER TWO

PREFECT

MASTER THREE

JUNIOR TWO

BOY PLAYING PIANO

TWEEDY WOMAN

PARENTS

DRIVER THREE

1. EXT. DAY

The cloistered buildings of a major public school. A young boy, seemingly sewn into his uniform, gazes dreamily upwards in the early spring sunshine. He lingers, dragging his feet on the flag-stones of the courtyard. Suddenly he is aware of the quick eyes of several groups of lordly, older ambling boys and he quickens his pace mechanically. He looks around him as if he had suddenly caught a scent of danger. Some boys pause and watch him. He quickens his pace again. The bell in the clock tower rings out as he turns smartly up the steps of the school and inside, beyond his observers.

2. INT. DAY

Inside the school, he hurries further still, avoiding the odd, curious glance from passing boys. At a large oak door he stops, knocks and enters.

3. INT. DAY

The headmaster's study. The HEAD *is talking to a young-to-middle-aged couple.*

HEAD: Ah, Jenkins. This is Mr. James Newbold.

JENKINS: How do you do, sir.

HEAD: Doubtless you will have heard of him. And Mrs. Newbold, his wife.

JENKINS: Yes, of course, sir.

HEAD: Mrs. Newbold is anxious to see a little more of the school before they have to leave. Will you see to it?

JENKINS: Yes, sir.

HEAD: I think you'll find Jenkins a pretty reliable guide—even if he's not the best historian.

9

(*Both somewhat aware of being dismissed.*)
It's been a great pleasure to meet you—and your wife too.
(*Ushering them out.*)
To be honest, I can't say I know your work well at first
hand . . . but I know many of the boys certainly do . . .
I'm sure they would have been most intrigued to meet you.
Jenkins, you are fortunate. . . .

JENKINS: Yes, sir.

MRS. NEWBOLD: Thank you, Headmaster. It's been quite
stimulating.

HEAD: So glad. Good-bye, again.

NEWBOLD: Good-bye.

JENKINS: This way, sir.

NEWBOLD: Right. Yes. Well, we'll follow you then. . . .
(*The door closes behind them.*)

4. INT. DAY

In the corridor they follow JENKINS *who soon becomes lost in reverie.*
NEWBOLD *is rather ill at ease and anxious to get away from the*
ritualized atmosphere. MRS. NEWBOLD *is in no hurry at all though*
and is aware of odd approving glances from passing boys.

5. EXT. DAY

Courtyard. They emerge from the main college buildings on to the
steps.

NEWBOLD: Well, thanks very much, er. . . .

JENKINS: Jenkins, sir.

NEWBOLD: Yes, well I think we'll get along before it, it gets
dark. Our car's waiting somewhere. Oh, there it is.

MRS. NEWBOLD: Don't be silly, darling. There's plenty of time.
Let's have another look around.

NEWBOLD: Really?

MRS. NEWBOLD: Yes, really. I want to see properly. After all,
it's important.

NEWBOLD: I'll say. I could do with a drink after that.

MRS. NEWBOLD: Well, they're not open yet. We can just take a
look round the playing fields and——

10

NEWBOLD: That'll be enough I should think.

MRS. NEWBOLD: We'll leave it to you, Jenkins. I'm sure you know your way round the school by now.

JENKINS: Very good, Mrs. Newbold. We could walk down to the nets. I'm I.C. of nets.

NEWBOLD: You're what?

MRS. NEWBOLD: In charge, dozy.

NEWBOLD: Well, I didn't go to one of these posh schools, did I?

MRS. NEWBOLD: You *didn't*.

JENKINS: And we could go through the chapel on the way if you'd like.

MRS. NEWBOLD: We'd like that very much.

(JENKINS *leads on dreamily. They follow some distance behind,* SHE *looking round with great interest,* HE *rather listless.*)

6. EXT. DAY

Chapel Cloisters. JENKINS *stops beside memorial to old boys killed in action. Hundreds of names. They gaze at the lists in silence.*

NEWBOLD: Both wars eh?

JENKINS: And the Boer, sir. They seem to have given up with Korea.

NEWBOLD: Just about used up the walls, I suppose.

JENKINS: Walls, sir?

NEWBOLD: What—seventeenth century is it?

JENKINS: Foundation laid by the Duke of Monmouth, sir.

NEWBOLD: Before he copped it?

JENKINS: Presumably, sir. All the roof and nave restored in rather florid, insensitive Victorian manner by C. K. Trilby about 1871–7.

NEWBOLD: Old boy?

JENKINS: Yes, sir.

(*As they pause before all this dullness,* NEWBOLD *tries to think of some insight but gives up as he sees his wife eyeing* JENKINS, *who is lost in his own thoughts again.*)

NEWBOLD: You don't fancy *him*, do you?

11

MRS. NEWBOLD: Of course.

NEWBOLD: I say—do you think this whole thing is such a good idea?

MRS. NEWBOLD: Don't be silly. It's the best idea we've ever had.

NEWBOLD: Let's take a butcher's at those blooming nets and then scoot off home. If you think you're talking me into this lot, you're crazy.

MRS. NEWBOLD: Don't be so narrow. Shall we go down to the nets?

(JENKINS *reawakens and they follow him.*)

7. EXT. DAY

Playing fields. Click of ball in the late afternoon light and so on. They watch the young figures. MRS. NEWBOLD *breathes in the air with pleasure.*

NEWBOLD: I'd forgotten what a really boring game it is. . . .

MRS. NEWBOLD: It's so *green* . . . um. . . .

NEWBOLD: *You* don't know one end from the other.
(*To* JENKINS) Do you play?

JENKINS: I'm sorry?

NEWBOLD: Cricket?

JENKINS: Just a bit. Not much good I'm afraid.

MRS. NEWBOLD: There you are, you see. You don't have to play if you don't want to.

NEWBOLD: Don't be silly. That's why you come to these places—to do things you'll never want to do again once you've left. . . .
(*They gaze at the scene as if it were a still-life, which, indeed, it seems to become.*)

8. EXT. DAY

Courtyard. They are saying good-bye to JENKINS—*still remote and polite.*

NEWBOLD: Very kind of you. I hope we haven't kept you from your homework—prep.

JENKINS (*dreamily*): It's been a pleasure to meet you, sir. And your wife. Goodbye, Mrs. Newbold.

MRS. NEWBOLD (*smiling*): It's been a pleasure to meet *you*.
(*They get into their hired car.* JENKINS *waits respectfully for them to go off. Once the car has moved off down the drive, he turns and makes his abstracted way back to the school.*)

9. EXT. DAY

School drive. The NEWBOLDS *sit in the car watching the buildings recede and the figures on the playing fields. All still. The chapel bell rings.*

NEWBOLD: I don't think that boy had all his marbles.

MRS. NEWBOLD: He's got more than his marbles all right. Relax. You'll get your drink in a minute. Think what you'd be like if you were *there*.

NEWBOLD: I am. That headmaster geezer was pretty patronizing.

MRS. NEWBOLD: I'm not surprised. Why did you look so nervous?

NEWBOLD: I can't help it. Those places give me the willies.

MRS. NEWBOLD: Oh, don't be boring again. I liked him. He was like my father's old headmaster.

NEWBOLD: Yes, and you know what your father told me—even the Japanese prison camp was better than *his* old school.

MRS. NEWBOLD: Well, I don't expect you'd have lasted five minutes with the Japs.

NEWBOLD: I'll bet I wouldn't.

MRS. NEWBOLD: Well, then!

NEWBOLD: Well, *what*?

MRS. NEWBOLD: Oh—nothing. . . .
(*They stare sulkily out of the windows. Pause.*)

NEWBOLD: Well, I'll tell you this now. We're not, repeat not, either of us going *there*. Besides I can't afford it. . . . Certainly not two of us. . . . (*Pause.*) So let's not waste any more time enquiring about it. . . . Shall we . . . ?
(*She refuses to respond. The* DRIVER *glances at them in his mirror.*)

DRIVER: Where to, sir?

NEWBOLD: Somewhere in the town for a decent meal.

MRS. NEWBOLD: *And* a drink.

13

NEWBOLD: You can't have one without the other really, you know.

MRS. NEWBOLD: I'm sure Jenkins can.

NEWBOLD: Well, good luck to him. Good luck to all of them. (*They stare back at the disappearing school buildings.*) They've got their future ahead of them.

MRS. NEWBOLD: So have we all—even if there is less of it. . . .

10. INT. NIGHT

Restaurant of county town pub. Somewhat pretentious and over-ambitious. The NEWBOLDS *are drinking a bottle of wine and finishing their dinner. In front of them they have piles of school prospectuses.*

MRS. NEWBOLD: I keep telling you I could get us into Eton easily.

NEWBOLD: And I keep telling you we're not going there.

MRS. NEWBOLD: My cousin could get us reduced fees in his House.

NEWBOLD: Apart from *us*, our children aren't going there.

MRS. NEWBOLD: If we ever have any children.

NEWBOLD: Quite. I mean why does anyone go through the whole thing? I mean they don't want *you*. Why should you want *them*? We're reasonably well off. Why should we lumber ourselves?

MRS. NEWBOLD: Don't tell me. When I think of it—nannies, rooms, trying to get away from them.

NEWBOLD: *Sending* them away.

MRS. NEWBOLD: Schools. . . .

NEWBOLD: No one sent me away.

MRS. NEWBOLD: Well, they should.

NEWBOLD: No they shouldn't. I should have been cherished at home. Not that I was. I hated it.

MRS. NEWBOLD: There you are.

NEWBOLD: So you keep saying. Well, we're supposed to be sending ourselves away now. And we're not going to that place this afternoon—even if you do fancy Jenkins.

MRS. NEWBOLD: Harrow.

NEWBOLD: Certainly not.

14

MRS. NEWBOLD: I'd look divine in those boaters.

NEWBOLD: Full of pushy spivs.

MRS. NEWBOLD: Try not to date yourself. . . . *They* went out with utility underwear.

NEWBOLD: One yank and they're off.

MRS. NEWBOLD: Yes, you could do with a bit of polish. Darling, you do live in the past—there aren't spivs any longer.

NEWBOLD: Oh yes there are: they make telly commercials, run men's boutiques and write scripts and things like that.

MRS. NEWBOLD: Wellington. I had an uncle there.

NEWBOLD: Yes, and what is he? In Germany with Nato. My career's behind me. And even if it weren't, it wouldn't be military.

MRS. NEWBOLD: Well, I'll tell you this, we're not going to one of those scruffy boy and girl places, where they all smoke and have affairs and call the teachers Alf and Mary.

NEWBOLD: No, I don't fancy that. Think who you'd meet. The parents I mean.

MRS. NEWBOLD: Poets who go round talking to young people, women who read the *Guardian*.

NEWBOLD: Women who *write* to the *Guardian*, complaining. . . .

MRS. NEWBOLD: Mothers who march for peace.

NEWBOLD: Alec D.

MRS. NEWBOLD: *Mrs.* Alec D.

NEWBOLD: Don't. . . .

MRS. NEWBOLD: All the people we flee from at home, coming down in *our* term time for Free Sessions. School jazz concerts, poetry evenings, drama sessions.

NEWBOLD: Know-ins, teach-ins.

MRS. NEWBOLD: Touch-ins. . . .

NEWBOLD: Go through that list again. . . . Do you know who went to Marlborough?

MRS. NEWBOLD: No—who?

NEWBOLD: Poor little devils. . . . What we want is somewhere in between. . . . There must be something. . . .

MRS. NEWBOLD: Of course.

NEWBOLD: Somewhere we can be free and easy, but enclosed,

but not harried or got at and pushed all the time. I don't
want to be pushed. I want to grow. . . .

MRS. NEWBOLD: Well, of course you will. And now you can
afford it.

NEWBOLD: Take the good. Able to respect the bad if you wish.
Free, left alone, able to develop your own personality, find
your own touchstone, but in some sort of traditional
landscape, pay lip-service-to-it-if-you-like, but no real
compromises or playing down. Be what you are. As well
as you can. Take advantage of *time*. While you can. Time
to read. Time to think. Make friendships. No matter if
they're not lasting. Better if they are. But. . . . Use your
body—if you want to. . . . Think about it all. Think about
love. The Past is still with you, it's not all gone forever.
The present is now and the future, the future's no more
than the ball thudding into the nets. And sleep afterwards.
Sleep like we've not known for years. . . .

MRS. NEWBOLD: What about this one?

NEWBOLD: What's that?

MRS. NEWBOLD: Crampton.

11. INT. DAY
C.U. Brochure of Crampton.

MRS. NEWBOLD (*V.O.*): Victorian, post-Arnold but humane,
open atmosphere. Emphasis on liberal arts, music, drama,
sculpture, courses in welding, as well as sciences,
technology, modern languages, laboratories, Russian a
school speciality. Religion Anglican but all denominations
welcome and open discussion on pressing subjects
encouraged. Hebrew lessons by arrangement. School
orchestra, debating society, jazz club, film society including
projected film maker's course. At present 430 pupils.
School colours, purple, white and orange. My favourite.
Darling, Crampton—let's give it a go!

12. EXT. DAY
Rolling grounds of Crampton. Buildings in distance.

16

13. Int. Day

Car Approaching Crampton. The NEWBOLDS *are in the back. He speaks to the* DRIVER.

NEWBOLD: Is this it? Is this Crampton?

DRIVER: This is Crampton School, sir.

NEWBOLD: Would you stop here? We'll walk the rest of the way. Oh, and pick us up, what would you say, darling— oh, at about 4.30.

DRIVER: Right you are, sir.

14. Ext. Day

Crampton grounds. The NEWBOLDS *alight from the car which reverses slowly in the drive. They walk towards the school. It is just evident for the first time that* MRS. NEWBOLD *is in an early stage of pregnancy. Only her husband is ever made to seem aware of it.*

MRS. NEWBOLD: Darling—

NEWBOLD: Yes?

MRS. NEWBOLD: I think this may just be it. What we're looking for.

NEWBOLD: Maybe you're right. . . . Hope so. At least it's not so blooming large . . . actually it's fairly small.

15. Ext. Day

Crampton buildings. They look up at the rather cosy Victorian Gothic pile. A boy approaches them.

BOY: May I help you, sir?

NEWBOLD: Oh, please. The Headmaster's house we're looking for.

BOY: This way, sir. If you'd care to follow. . . .

MRS. NEWBOLD: Beautiful manners.

NEWBOLD: Thank you.

(*They follow arm-in-arm.*)

16. Int. Day

Headmaster's study. Crampton. The Headmaster, MR. TESTER, *is talking to the* NEWBOLDS, *who are seated in front of his desk.*

TESTER: What we've tried to do here—and I'm not saying we've succeeded, but that's up to the people who come here as pupils, like yourselves—is to strike that elusive medium you've spoken about—very eloquently if I may say so, Newbold.

NEWBOLD: Well . . .

TESTER: Too many regard what is no more than innovation as revolution. Others regard tradition as the only defence left against technology and becoming themselves mere objects in the super politics of the new communication. Crampton is not that. Crampton is for the human, the particular, the eccentric, the concrete, the special, the worst of the best and the best of the worst. . . .

NEWBOLD: I was wondering about privacy . . .

TESTER: We pursue it.

NEWBOLD: Oh, good. I mean a separate room to work in . . .

TESTER: That is part of the Crampton way. But you shall see.

NEWBOLD: I mean my wife, I mean. Pauline here.

TESTER: Yes. Mrs. Newbold. Let's see . . . Pauline.

MRS. NEWBOLD: Pauline Laura.

TESTER: Father's name?

MRS. NEWBOLD: Mellor.

TESTER: Mellor . . . P. L. . . . You know the fees of course, Mr. Newbold. Extras: music, Russian and so on. . . .

NEWBOLD: Well, I don't think Russian anyway.

TESTER: I should think you'd both be sailing through three, four "A" Levels by next summer term.

NEWBOLD: Well, you see, my . . . Newbold . . . Mellor, she's . . .

MRS. NEWBOLD: I took Higher School Certificate in six subjects, four distinctions in 1940.

TESTER: Yes, it's all here. And you, Newbold, Newbold . . .

NEWBOLD: James, Arthur . . . Newbold.

TESTER: I see you took the Oxford School Certificate in five subjects, four, what, credits and a pass. No mathematics.

NEWBOLD: No.

TESTER: Well, we shall see.

NEWBOLD: I left then . . . I would have liked to go to the university but I didn't have the subjects and it was the

18

war and my mother was out at work.

MRS. NEWBOLD: Perhaps we should take a look at the studies. The school is looking quite beautiful from here, Headmaster.

TESTER: Doesn't it? I love this time of day. This time of year.

NEWBOLD: I was rather a, well, a late developer.

TESTER: We have them all here, Newbold. . . . Late developers and all the rest. That's our little secret. I think we shall get you together with your Housemasters. I think you, Mellor, Macready's probably best suited for you and they need fresh blood at present. And you, er, er Newbold—I think Grant's. Grant's House. Plenty of adventure there but still room to stretch your own self, *your* personality. Going through an odd patch at present. But the Head of House, Heffer, yes, Heffer, forceful, imaginative boy, thoughtful. Ah—Groom, Shippard, do come in.

(GROOM *and* SHIPPARD, *Housemasters of Macready's and Grant's respectively enter.* NOTE: *at no time does anyone, including staff or boys, seem aware of the age, sex or relation of the* NEWBOLDS. *They are new boys.*)

TESTER: I want you to meet two new recruits for Macready's and Grant's. Newbold . . .

NEWBOLD: How do you do—sir.

SHIPPARD: Good evening, Newbold.

TESTER: And Mellor.

MRS. NEWBOLD: How do you do, sir.

GROOM: Evening, young Mellor.

TESTER: I think the Fourth for Newbold. And—oh, Lower Fifth for, er, er Mellor. At least on the basis of what we, we seem to have gleaned. Anyhow, I leave it to you gentlemen. Let them settle in to their respective houses and we'll see how they scrum down.

GROOM: I think you can leave them to us all right, Headmaster.

SHIPPARD: Think we could both do with a bit of fresh blood.

GROOM: Me more than you. So: welcome to Upton, young Mellor.

MRS. NEWBOLD: *Thank* you, sir.

GROOM: *And*, welcome to Macready's. You've actually landed the best House.

SHIPPARD: Nonsense, Newbold's got the best House. I hope he deserves it. It's rather up to him, Headmaster. Yes?

TESTER: It's up to them both. To do the best they can. For Crampton and themselves.

SHIPPARD: Well, Newbold, let's get you settled in eh? I expect you're a bit tired, journey, new faces and all that stuff. I'll show you round the House a bit before you turn in. You'll find you'll have a pretty heavy day tomorrow.

GROOM: And I'll take you over to Macready's. Let me help you with your things.

MRS. NEWBOLD: Oh no, sir, I can manage.

GROOM: Oh, well, I imagine the porter will manage with them both.

SHIPPARD: Goodnight, Headmaster.

TESTER: Goodnight all of you. Do your best. I'll do mine. Leave the rest to Crampton.

(*They go out.* TESTER *lights his pipe dreamily and stares out at the towers of Crampton.*)

17. EXT. NIGHT

Crampton. Courtyard. SHIPPARD *and* GROOM *take their separate charges to their Houses.*

SHIPPARD: 'Night Groom. Luck of the draw again.

GROOM: Hard luck. Still—never know . . .

SHIPPARD: *I* know—usually. Come along, Newbold, you'll be in time for some cocoa if we get a move on.

(NEWBOLD *exchanges glances with his wife, who follows* GROOM, *shrugging fairly cheerfully. He watches her glumly, then, clutching his bags, stumbles after* SHIPPARD.)

18. INT. NIGHT

Crampton. NEWBOLD'S *bedroom. He finishes unpacking under the bare light of his room. Tries to jolly it up a bit with photographs (including one of his wife), books, radio, etc. Cleans his teeth, turns back and winces slightly at the cold touch of the sheets on the bed. He gets a bottle of whisky from his case, pours himself one out into a tooth-glass, turns out the light and stares out of the window at the school buildings, in the cold moonlight, the odd light beaming from a corridor.*

19. INT. NIGHT
Crampton. MRS. NEWBOLD'S *bedroom. She hangs up lots of dresses and puts clothes in chests of drawers. Takes out her tennis racket. Removes her make-up quickly, sips at a glass of milk, grasps a hot-water bottle to her, snuggles gratefully into bed and turns out the light.*

20. INT. NIGHT
Crampton. Courtyard. Bell from the chapel rings out. Silence. From his window, NEWBOLD *stares out thoughtfully, smoking a cigar.*

21. INT. DAY
Crampton. NEWBOLD'S *bedroom. He is asleep in bed. A boy, about sixteen, looks down at him and examines his cold cigar butt and glass of whisky. Bells are sounding everywhere and the noise of feet and voices.* NEWBOLD *stirs. He winces and reacts to the grinning face looking down at him.*
NEWBOLD: Who are you?
BOY: Who are *you*?
NEWBOLD: Newbold. Where am I?
BOY: Grant's. Crampton. Remember? Newbold what?
NEWBOLD: Newbold what? What are you talking about?
BOY: Names.
NEWBOLD: Oh. James. James Arthur.
BOY: Newbold. N.J. All right, Newbold. You'd better get your skates on. It's ten past seven.
NEWBOLD: Seven! Oh—I've got a headache.
BOY: Well, I wouldn't go to Matron with it. She'll smell your breath and send you straight to Head of House. Welcome to good old Grant's, Newbold.
   (*He rips the clothes off the bed.*)
BOY: It won't be the worst time of your life. And it sure won't be the best.

21

(*He switches on* NEWBOLD'S *radio to pop music and goes out.*
NEWBOLD *turns it off and looks around helplessly.*)

22. INT. DAY
Crampton. Wash-changing-room. NEWBOLD *stumbles about in some
embarrassment among the showers, basins and milling boys in their
pyjamas. He either avoids looking at them in some guilty way or
tries to look friendly. Neither approach works at all. Most of the
House have already left. He has brought his electric shaver but sees
there is no plug for it. Sensibly he has also brought a safety razor
which he starts to use. He turns to one of the few boys left.*
NEWBOLD: What time's breakfast then?
BOY: Now. And we've had it!
    (*He skips out.*)

23. INT. DAY
Crampton. Shower. NEWBOLD *turns the lever marked* "hot". *It comes
out relentlessly cold. He dunks small portions of himself, looks to
see if he's observed, and, seeing that he is the last there, stumbles
off to his room.*

24. INT. DAY
*Dining hall. Grant's. The place is packed with boys, aged thirteen to
sixteen. Mostly fairly silent but eating the remains of breakfast
fairly hard. A few heads look up. Mild amusement or indifference.
He goes to a long table for his breakfast. Helps himself to a little
of the debris, takes tea from a strange urn and finally looks for a
seat. Eventually, a boy leaves his place but clearly because he'd
rather leave anyway.* NEWBOLD *stares down at his plate, sips his tea.
He is dressed like all the other boys. Perhaps a bit too carefully.*

25. INT. DAY
A young boy approaches him. He looks quite tiny, making NEWBOLD
more of a stunted giant than ever.
TINY: Newbold?
NEWBOLD: Er. Yes. You?
TINY: You're to see Heffer.

NEWBOLD: Heffer who?

TINY: Head of House. After Chapel. And *right* after, mind.

NEWBOLD: Where?

TINY: In his room, where do you think? Downtown Chicago?

26. EXT. DAY

Crampton. Courtyard. Boys and staff are emerging from everywhere.
NEWBOLD *is wondering whom he can ask the way to the chapel.*
They all seem preoccupied, ignoring him. Suddenly he sees his wife
dressed in a gym slip, otherwise in the school colours of her favourite
purple, white and orange. He waves at her thankfully but she is deep
in conversation with a couple of boys. He follows her and eventually
finds himself in the entrance to the chapel, jostled by hundreds of
boys.

27. INT. DAY

School chapel. NEWBOLD *stumbles about despairingly for a place to*
merge into the sea of boys. No one seems to notice him until an
initiated looking junior boy nods him towards a place near the door.
As the psalm commences, he looks around for his wife. He catches
sight of her pretty head bowed over her prayer book, thinking how
attractive she looks in these odd surroundings, he tries to catch her
attention. A few cold stares result from those who notice. The boy
beside him finally nudges him as if he were being friendly. He smiles
back but the response is quickly shut off. He hears TESTER'S *voice*
rumbling.

TESTER: . . . as it is the beginning of yet another new term, I
will not waste your time or mine on reflection or speculation.
Holidays, with their undoubted pleasures are come and
gone, past, school is here once again. In your case, and
mine, Crampton is here. The world will not wait on us long.
And, indeed, we do not expect it, nor shall it. Your school
stands as we do at this time. Your Houses await you. To
those of you who are new amongst us and no doubt feeling
strange and unfamiliar with our ways, I say welcome to
you—to each and all of you—on behalf of each and all of us.
That is to say, Crampton. Our ways will be yours in a very short

23

time and you will find it hard to believe you knew any other. May the Lord bless and keep us in all we strive honestly and fairly to do, whatever that outcome may be. Let us bless the good grace that watches over us and enables us to go about our ways here in the midst of a troubled, divided and waning world. A world full of suspicion, misery, faction and injustice. Let us remember at all times who we are and what we set out here to do, however humble or ordinary it may seem to be. Through Jesus Christ our Lord, in the name of the Father and the Holy Ghost. . . . Mr. Groom would like to see all boys before Second School who have access to keys of the language laboratory. During term-time, of course. That is, boys from all Houses naturally. I think we shall sing Arthur Clough's hymn "Say Not the Struggle Naught Availeth". You have the number. May not be how any of us would put it today but still—I shouldn't fault it for that. No. . . .

(*The School sings the hymn. During it,* NEWBOLD *manages finally to get his wife's attention. She smiles back at him happily and sings sweetly.*)

28. EXT. DAY

Crampton. The school piles out of chapel. NEWBOLD *struggles to contact his wife but she is caught up in a crowd and carried off, chattering.*

29. INT. DAY

HEFFER'S *study.* HEFFER, *Head of House, who is a bit of an eccentric, about seventeen, but honest in his way, is addressing* NEWBOLD.

HEFFER: The thing about this place is that it's not really one thing nor the other. But what is? Where is? It's not bloody Winchester or Manchester G.S. even. It's not one of those stale holes and it's not one of Evelyn Waugh's jokes. The blokes here—and by that I mean staff too—are as good as anywhere and just as mediocre and bloody awful. But you're here now, though looking at you, God knows why. You're Crampton and Crampton's you and all that crap Tester talks in Chapel. But what matters to me—and that means it's number

24

one in your book of anything—is that you're in my House
—Grant's—and that delicate, mysterious, brooding,
unlovely, superb mechanism is the real you now. It is like
the body of Christ. It inhabits you and you inhabit it. Now
—where's your room?

NEWBOLD: "D" Landing. No. 7.

HEFFER: "D" Landing! You're not in some army factory farm,
preparing you for a man's life in the new expanding
world of weapons and technology. It's corridor "D".

NEWBOLD: I see.

HEFFER: You will call me sir at all times and other various
personages about whom you will learn in double bloody
alarming time. You're neither in a doss house for scruffy-
minded *New Statesman* wet eggs or the offspring of fecund
women graduates and breast fed from Aldermaston to Gros-
venor bloody Square. You will come to me here—or where-
ever-I-happen-to-be—and you'll find me—every morning
after Chapel until I tell you not to—and report. It's a daft
system, the whole thing but so is the Divine bloody Office,
and the democratic process, one man one vote, the techno-
logical revolution where even the tin-openers don't work let
alone the money system and workers and industry and the
thoughts of Chairman bloody Mao. I'm not asking for your
agreement, Newbold. Your views are of no interest to
anyone and I doubt if they ever will be, even at Crampton. You
will not cook your own food, drink, bet, smoke—either
old-fashioned tobacco or pot, you will *run* during the hours
of daylight in the House—*but* making no noise. You will
wear the correct tie—which I see you are not—at the
correct times, you will not sing, whistle, put your hands in
your pockets, wear a waistcoat, use hair oil or cream,
neither make nor respond to homosexual advances. You will
not join any club or society, cultural, social or political until
such time as you are invited or given permission by your
Head of House, that is to say, me. Clear?

NEWBOLD: Not quite, sir.

HEFFER: It will be. You'll find out—we're not bloody Germans,

25

you know. Plundering efficiency queens. This place may be chaos, Newbold, chaos to you, even to me, but it's bloody human.

NEWBOLD: Yes, sir. I see that.

HEFFER: And what is that place?

NEWBOLD: Upton, sir.

HEFFER: It's not bloody Crampton. It's Grant's. Let me tell you about your House, Newbold. I will not even try to explain the instinct, let alone the thinking, behind the House System —as it exists within the school. Look to history for that, Newbold, and as I doubt you will be able to look to that, you being what you probably are and the world what it quite clearly is, look to yourself if you dare or care to, and, perhaps, one day, one moment of one, idiotic irrational, mocked and ritualized day, a harsh and unwelcome glint of what I mean will stop you in the course of whatever ridiculous task you have been set to do, and, if life has been kind to you at all or ever will be, that harshness will be as sweet, lovely and momentous as a Damascus jerk-off to you. I hope so, though I must tell you, at first glance, and— oh—well, it seems unlikely. But—Newbold—but—oh, the House. The system. Why are we here, what are we for and all that balls, do forget it. At least, forget it while you are here . . . at Grant's. Nation does not speak unto Nation, say whatever Reith or Lord Hill or *The Times Literary Supplement* (*try* not to use shorteners—*that's* one itself. Like that boy from St. John's Wood who goes to see "The Don" at Glyndebourne. I wouldn't go there if I were you anyway, Newbold. Probably ever. You'd be—oh—the Town Choral Society, Handel Society—*Julius Caesar*—or "*Hercules*". One of those.) What happened? Ah. No: commiseration—loves not nor cares not nor knows not not wot not about its fellow conurbation. They will tell you we are living on no more than a concrete airstrip on a four-hour flight to Paris, France from New York. Heed them not. They are the hangdogs and harbingers of no more than the noisy gang bangs of the twenty-first century—about

26

which, less later. Planet speaks not to planet, earth not to earth, nation not to nation and man—not—not, we say, to man. If you don't see it, doubtless you never shall and if you do, it will finally astonish me. Except that I don't wish to add to my daily quota of disappointment. House enjoins House. It is pathetic, outmoded, full of misery and joyous energy. . . .

(*He goes into a reverie.*)

NEWBOLD: A friend of mine——

HEFFER: What?

NEWBOLD: Another . . . new boy . . . is in Macready's.

HEFFER: Macready's. Well, I suppose you might as well be put into the picture about the other Houses at Crampton. Though why I should do it, I don't know. Except that you seem unusually dim for a new boy, even in my untypical experience. Newbold, there are several Houses here at Crampton, of which only really six need concern you. The rest are of such additional awfulness, such runts, such after-thoughts, they are the change of life babies of all creation and not even to be regarded, just discreetly avoided. First there is Grant's. Then Macready's. Then, what are known as the Histories: Salisbury, Buckingham, Percy and Northumberland—our founder, the Reverend Pearce being a rather martial-minded cleric and keen on Shakespeare and England, in that order. Which was no doubt pretty shrewd of him, don't you agree? You are not expected to reply or express an opinion. You have none nor probably ever will do. You are a ready-to-wear number, you will mumble on quick daily services between Big Block corridor "D" to Semi-Block avenue "D". Very well, take note for I'll not tell you again. Houses: Macready's: maximum effort, but too much in the past. But lots of rather depressing and apparently successful results.

NEWBOLD: That's where my friend——

HEFFER: Who? Did you say something?

NEWBOLD: My—friend.

27

HEFFER: Your friend? I hope you're not looking forward to any romantic attachment, Newbold. Especially to someone in Macready's. If you are, let me tell you now, you're in for a sad time. Because I'll see it comes to nothing; understand?

NEWBOLD: Yes—sir.

HEFFER: What's your friend's name?

NEWBOLD: Mellor, sir.

HEFFER: Mellor *what*?

NEWBOLD: *What*? Oh—Mellor, P. L.

HEFFER: Mellor, P. L. I'll keep a look out for that one. I'm not having anyone in Grant's having affairs with Macready's. Come to that, I'm not having *any* affairs in Grant's if I can help it. Except in special cases and I don't know what they might be except for established marriages about which one can do really nothing without bringing the House into ridicule. It makes only for a climate of rivalry, bitchiness and treachery. Anyway, I won't have it. As for heterosexual affairs, there's not much scope there apart from Matron, the Housemaster's wife, who is five foot two and weighs ten stone and has moles on her face and permanently-stained armpits. The Head's secretary's wife is a nymphomaniac but she is too booked up and busy to be likely to be interested in the likes of you. As I was saying:

30. EXT. DAY

(*V.O.*) *Macready's House. Including* MRS. NEWBOLD.

HEFFER: Macready's is smug and academically brilliant. They have a smart but basically unsophisticated sense of what is style, which they are busy putting on all the time, making easy things look difficult and difficult things easy, and manage to fool most of the school most of the time.

31. INT. DAY

HEFFER'S *study*.

HEFFER: Full of great one-shot intellectual energies but no genuine stamina. Salisbury: this is about as dowdy as you can get.

28

32. EXT. DAY

(V.O.) Salisbury House. Boys.

HEFFER: This lot are the real worked-on ones. They don't know
if they're on the telly or off it. No real identity at all but
jerking off all the time trying to explain themselves to
themselves. Think they're great on liturgy, and a lot of
pathetic showing-off about that but no real feeling for it,
let alone knowledge. They're great at games simply because
they *try* so depressingly hard. Lots of beefy hand-holding
and buggery. Buckingham: frightfully worthy. Try to
pretend they're at a different sort of place altogether from
Crampton: free-wheeling, now I'll tell you where their premise
is wrong, that sociology is the only *real* science, because it's
also art and it's also political.

33. INT. DAY

HEFFER'S *study.*

HEFFER: They're so permissive they're wild about themselves.
But the truth is they're more repressive, fascist and
mean-minded in all their rule-breaking, they'd break your
heart in a week. Percy: oldest House of all and will they
stop reminding you.

34. EXT. DAY

Percy House. Boys. Masters.

HEFFER *(V.O.)*: Not that it's of any interest as the building is as
undistinguished as its scholars, having produced no one in
a hundred years but a back-bench buffoon who excites
them to death about himself every prize-giving, and their
prize star, a Bishop, the controversial—if that's what you
call being potty—author of *A Docker Talks to God.* The
Bishop himself, of course, being more keen on young
dockers than old Gods. Goody-goody, dull, naïve but
brutal, competitive like only the most inspired mediocrities,
they'd all like Vanessa Redgrave to be their mother and
visit them on Speech Day.

35. INT. DAY

HEFFER: I hope you're making note of this because my assessment is impeccable as well as ineffable and I shall test you in your reactions to each of the other Houses in the next ten days when you've cast your very small, bloodshot eyes over them. I hope that's not drink. Northumberland:

36. EXT. DAY

Northumberland House.

HEFFER (*V.O.*): Last House of all to end this uneventful history. Amiable lot. In some ways, probably the best one for you if you'd not got shoved on to me. Friendly crowd, most opportunity to be spontaneous without exhibitionism and eccentricity. Tolerant but a lot of scepticism around, perhaps too much, so therefore a little lacking in confidence and consequently pockets of rather Woman's Hour Neurosis. Steady workers, some above average material but prone to fits of rather absurd depression and defeatism. A lot due to Housemaster's lunacy and self-obsession.

37. INT. DAY

HEFFER'S *study*.

HEFFER: As for Grant's, well you shall find out. It's not what it should be. But it can be and I'm going to see to it. So will you. It should be quite an exercise in discovery for you. And remember what I said about sex. Keep away from the maids and pretty boys. As for pulling your wire, that's no occupation for a gentleman, though as you're in Grant's, the likelihood of your being a gentleman is pretty remote. In this House "B" is for boy and "F" is for effort. You may go now.

NEWBOLD: Thank you, sir.

HEFFER: What's your name?

NEWBOLD: Name, sir? Newbold. I mean James, sir. I mean. Newbold, J. A.

(HEFFER *nods dismissal.*)

38. INT. DAY

Outside HEFFER'S *study.* NEWBOLD *closes the door. He looks
thoroughly at sea.*

HEFFER (*V.O.*): Impeccable and ineffable . . . impeccable and
    ineffable . . .

39. INT. DAY

MATRON'S *room.* NEWBOLD *being dosed by* MATRON.

40. EXT. DAY

Evening. School courtyard. Still bewildered, NEWBOLD *walks alone.
The clock tower chimes. He approaches a senior boy.*

NEWBOLD: Excuse me, would you tell me please where is
    Macready's House?
    (*The senior boy hardly glances at him and walks past. A
    Junior boy grins at the surprised* NEWBOLD.)

JUNIOR: New boys don't address seniors unless they're spoken
    to first. And when you're spoken to, you jump.

NEWBOLD: It's a bit difficult to pick up the rules all at once.

JUNIOR: It's not difficult. It's bloody impossible.

NEWBOLD: Well, yes, and unfair.

JUNIOR: That's the way it is.

NEWBOLD: You can tell me where Macready's House is? Or is
    that not allowed?

JUNIOR: You haven't got time. It's chapel now. You'd better
    get a move on. Anyway, they don't like you Grant's lot
    hanging around Macready's.

NEWBOLD: But I've got a . . . I mean there's a friend. . . .

JUNIOR: I should keep away from Macready's if you don't
    want a quick duffing-up.
    (*He walks away to the chapel.*)

41. INT. NIGHT

Chapel. The School sings a hymn. NEWBOLD *tries to catch his wife's
eye but she's joining in blandly. She looks as content as he is uneasy.*

31

HEFFER (*reads aloud*): O Lord our Heavenly Father, Thou hast
promised the Holy Spirit to those who ask. Mercifully
forgive me all my sins and prepare my heart and the hearts
of all who are seeking with me, that we may receive Thy
great Gift. Grant me to do Thy will all through life and in
devoted service glorify Thy Holy Name, being faithful
unto death. Bless and inspire those who minister to us, and
all who pray for us. Through Jesus our Lord and Saviour.
Amen.

42. EXT. NIGHT

Chapel. NEWBOLD *tries to catch up with his wife. He calls out to her.
She turns, smiles, rather vaguely and waves, is caught up in a crowd
of boys who are all chatting. She looks full of energy, initiative—
unlike her husband. Her new House companions stare coldly. Then
usher her on chummily—not a pretty boy. Or even a thirtyish
woman.* NEWBOLD *watches her cross the square, with its green and
Victorian Gothic, and then walks off on his own.*

NEWBOLD (*V.O.*): Psalm, hymn, lesson . . . stand up for
yourself . . . mix with all kinds . . . learn responsibility . . .
psalm, hymn, lesson, mix with all kinds. . . . Export or
die . . . tighten our belts . . . increased efficiency . . .
efficiency . . . methods . . . new methods . . . expand . . .
develop . . . innovate . . . development. . . . You see . . . I
feel . . . I *feel* . . . young. . . .

(*His figure recedes, becomes small and merges with the
background.*)

43. INT. NIGHT

NEWBOLD'S *room. He tries to read in bed. Looks at his wife's
photograph. Turns out the light. Light from the School. The clock
chimes.*

44. INT. DAY

NEWBOLD'S *room. Bell. He gets out of bed. As if for years.*

45. INT. DAY

Shower room. NEWBOLD. *Last. Steam and cold.*

46. INT. DAY
Dining hall. NEWBOLD *walks in. Ignored. He finds a place at his table and looks across at a row of removed faces. One faintly friendly one looks back. His name is Partridge. About fifteen.* NEWBOLD *looks at his breakfast.*

PARTRIDGE: Good old baked beans! Where would we be
    without 'em? What would we be?

NEWBOLD: Yes. . . .

    (NEWBOLD *looks at his breakfast rather gratefully.*)

47. INT. DAY
Chapel. School at prayer.

NEWBOLD (*V.O.*): Psalm, hymn, lesson. . . . Actually . . . it's not
    too bad . . . is it?

    (*He looks for his wife. She is absorbed in the service.*)

48. EXT. DAY
Courtyard. Boys hurrying from chapel to morning school. NEWBOLD *watches his wife with her new friends but makes no effort to follow her.* PARTRIDGE *nudges him.*

PARTRIDGE: Double period maths. You'll *hate* it. Come on.

    (*He links arms. They walk to morning school.*)

49. INT. DAY
Classroom. The Maths Master is staring down at NEWBOLD *on his feet.*

MATHS MASTER: What is your name?

NEWBOLD: Newbold—J. A.—sir.

MASTER: Newbold—*If* you don't understand the question, and
    you clearly don't, don't attempt an answer.

    (NEWBOLD *sits down.*)

50. EXT. DAY
Yard. NEWBOLD *wanders on his own. Everywhere boys. Suddenly his wife. But no one seems to notice them. Except* PARTRIDGE.

PARTRIDGE: Bad luck about that.

NEWBOLD: Oh, well, I suppose that's what it's going to be like.

PARTRIDGE: I was at a co-ed school before. Boarding, progressive. You know?

NEWBOLD: Yes?

PARTRIDGE: Oh—you know: pets, women. Free and easy, etcetera. No chapel. No games if you didn't like 'em. Cinema, weekends what you want. Call the staff by their first names. Any clothes you like. Jeans . . . everybody . . . what a funny word . . . Jeans . . . girls wore jewellery if they wanted. Rotten jewellery. No one talked about work. Not like here. Oh—politics. Sociology. Things. Like that. Well: we *did* things. Did. Like, oh—music and art. Pottery. Engineering. Oh, things—like that. And then there were less intellectual things. Films. Plays. Dancing. . . .

51. EXT. DAY

School grounds. PARTRIDGE *and* NEWBOLD *walking. They watch boys at nets.*

PARTRIDGE: You could do what you like. I suppose. But it was a bit, you know, like everyone knew it wasn't for real. Sort of acting—acting *not* being at school. Still—it was fun some of the time. And you could always *skip* a class. Always. And not get into the steaming merde like here. There was a lot of uniform really. You get *noticed* here. . . . We're all dressed the same but different . . . I mean—look at Johnstone . . .

52. INT. DAY

School nets.

PARTRIDGE (*V.O.*): Peppard . . . Rose . . . Davies. . . . They're all names. Names.

53. INT. DAY

Classroom.

MASTER: Newbold.

NEWBOLD: Sir?

MASTER: Construe.
NEWBOLD: Sir?
MASTER: Would you construe, Newbold?
NEWBOLD: Yes, sir. . . .
    (*He clears his throat.*)

54. INT. DAY
Dining hall. NEWBOLD *finds his way. He is ignored except by* PARTRIDGE. HEFFER *watches. He looks down at his food.*

55. INT. DAY
Classroom. A Master is speaking soundlessly. NEWBOLD *stares out of the window. Suddenly his wife appears on a tennis court. He watches her in action. He watches others watching her.*
MASTER: Newbold!
NEWBOLD: Sir?
MASTER: Treaty of Utrecht.
NEWBOLD: 1712.
MASTER: That's hardly an answer. . . . What else?

56. INT. DAY
Classroom. NEWBOLD *watches his wife serve.*

57. EXT. DAY
Playing fields. NEWBOLD *and* PARTRIDGE. *They are watching a scrum-down.*
NEWBOLD: Why do they make us watch it?
PARTRIDGE: If you can't do it—you watch it.

58. INT. DAY
NEWBOLD'S *room.* NEWBOLD *and* PARTRIDGE *having a fry-up.*
NEWBOLD: Good old baked beans!
HEFFER (*V.O.*): Newbold!
PARTRIDGE: Jump! I'll keep 'em warm.
    (NEWBOLD *jumps.*)

59. INT. NIGHT

School. NEWBOLD *at prep.* HEFFER *presiding.*

NEWBOLD (*V.O.*): He's right . . . I don't understand the
    questions. . . .
    (HEFFER *watches him.*)

NEWBOLD (*V.O.*): God . . . the B.O. . . . I'll say this for him—
    he hasn't got it . . . the bad breath . . . socks . . . where is
    she? Damn bloody Macready's. . . . They've all done it—
    all except me . . . I'm behind. . . .
    (HEFFER *still watches him as he struggles with his prep.*)

60. INT. NIGHT

NEWBOLD'S *room. He looks at his wife's picture. Turns out the*
light.

NEWBOLD: Again!
    (*He turns over.*)

60A. INT. DAY

Sanatorium. MATRON'S *room.* MRS. NEWBOLD *in schoolboy striped*
pyjamas is having her temperature taken. Her tummy is a crescent
profile in dormitory flannel. MATRON *whips the thermometer out of*
her mouth. MRS. NEWBOLD *looks bored.* MATRON *shakes the instru-*
ment briskly after examining it.

MATRON: You'll do. Nothing out of the ordinary for you,
    Mellor. Fresh air and hard work's the best pick-me-up for
    all of us.

MRS. NEWBOLD: Yes, Matron. Can I go now, please?

MATRON: Get along then. Next?
    (*Boy similarly clad to* MRS. NEWBOLD *advances to the*
    shaking thermometer.)
    Bowels?
    (MRS. NEWBOLD *skips out.*)

61. EXT. DAY

Local town. Rather dull place. Not much character. NEWBOLD *looks*
in all the shops. Every kind. He tries to look anonymous and goes
into the local Italianate Hotel.

62. INT. DAY

Inn. MRS. NEWBOLD, *looking like a housewife of the district, is waiting at a table. Her husband joins her.*[1]

63. INT. DAY

Inn.

NEWBOLD: It was a mistake all right. A real mistake.

MRS. NEWBOLD: Do you think so?

NEWBOLD: Yes. Yes. I jolly well do. Don't you?

MRS. NEWBOLD: I don't know.

NEWBOLD: Well, I do.

MRS. NEWBOLD: I'm not sure.

NEWBOLD: They watch you. You fit in. *And* they watch you. They watch you. Looking up your skirt when you're playing tennis.

MRS. NEWBOLD: Oh, really?

NEWBOLD: Yes—really. . . . I miss you.

MRS. NEWBOLD: I miss *you*.

NEWBOLD: You don't seem to.

MRS. NEWBOLD: But I do.

(*Pause.*)

NEWBOLD: Well, I don't think I'm doing very well. In fact, I know I'm not doing very well. Grant's. Well—they'd be glad to see the back of me all right. The Head of House. Everybody. Even little Partridge.

MRS. NEWBOLD: Oh, yes. I've seen you with him. Is that his name? Partridge.

NEWBOLD: How is Macready's?

MRS. NEWBOLD: Well—I hate to say it. But I think it *is* the best.

NEWBOLD: Yes. . . . Heffer's awfully good in his way.

MRS. NEWBOLD: So I hear.

NEWBOLD: I miss you. I just—well I just miss you.

MRS. NEWBOLD: I miss you.

NEWBOLD: Not in the same way, I think.

MRS. NEWBOLD: Oh, yes. In the same way.

[1] In this scene, NEWBOLD is especially aware of his wife's physically self-absorbed condition. He is as tentative as she is contained.

NEWBOLD: I'm not doing very well.

MRS. NEWBOLD: I'm sorry. The term's only half through.

NEWBOLD: It won't . . . it won't improve.

MRS. NEWBOLD: Of course it will. . . . It all takes time.

> (*She takes his hand.*)
>
> Don't despair. Let's drink to Grant's.

NEWBOLD: O.K. And, Macready's.

MRS. NEWBOLD: Grant's and Macready's.

> (*She kisses his cheek. He looks around at the other customers.*)

64. EXT. DAY

Playing fields. NEWBOLD *and his wife walking past boys playing rugger.*

NEWBOLD: I do miss you. . . .

MRS. NEWBOLD: I miss you. I told you.

NEWBOLD: How's Macready's?

MRS. NEWBOLD: Rather good I think. Really rather good.

NEWBOLD: Grant's is difficult. I seem to have struck a bad patch. . . .

MRS. NEWBOLD: So I hear. . . .

NEWBOLD: I really do miss you. . . .

MRS. NEWBOLD: I know. . . . I told you. . . .

NEWBOLD: You're doing very well. Aren't you?

MRS. NEWBOLD: Well—perhaps it's easier for me. Macready's is good of course.

NEWBOLD: Of course? Is it?

MRS. NEWBOLD: Yes. . . .

> (*They watch the players.*)

NEWBOLD: What a game.

MRS. NEWBOLD: Oh—it's all right.

NEWBOLD: *You* don't play it.

MRS. NEWBOLD: No. . . . Neither do you.

NEWBOLD: I'm not up to it. I don't want to get hurt. Why should I?

MRS. NEWBOLD: Indeed.

NEWBOLD: Why should we? Darling? I *do* miss . . . sorry . . .

boring. . . . Why *are* we?

MRS. NEWBOLD: Well—it doesn't matter.

NEWBOLD: I can't keep up. I can't keep up. You're on *Horace*.
I know. Me—*Julius Caesar*.

MRS. NEWBOLD: The common herd of men——

NEWBOLD: I know—except I don't. I keep them far at bay.
Let's go. I'll lay on a hired car. We can go home. . . . I
want you. . . . I didn't know. Something is wrong. . .

MRS. NEWBOLD: I'm——

NEWBOLD: What? I'm?

MRS. NEWBOLD: Nothing. Society. Meeting and addressing
it. . . .

NEWBOLD: I want you.

MRS. NEWBOLD: I know. It's all a bit strange isn't it?

NEWBOLD: Can I come and see you?

MRS. NEWBOLD: Grant's are not exactly *persona grata* at
Macready's.

NEWBOLD: I know. . . . Can I?

MRS. NEWBOLD: I think . . . I really do think—we must see it—
through.
(*She pats his hand.*)
Learn . . . learn patience.
(*She walks away from him. Someone's head is scrunched in
the scrum. His eyes follow her.*)

65. EXT. DAY

Playing fields. HEFFER *comes up to* NEWBOLD.

HEFFER: You'll watch. I'll see to that. You'll always watch.
You're not good enough to take part. You'll never be in
any team this House ever had. But you'll watch. By God,
you'll watch, Newbold. I'll see to that.
(*He goes off.* NEWBOLD *watches. Then the game.*)

66. INT. DAY

NEWBOLD'S *room. He comes into it. It has been wrecked.* PARTRIDGE
comes in, looks around at the desolation and sits down.

39

67. EXT. DAY

Local town. NEWBOLD *and* PARTRIDGE *wander about the dreary, characterless town.*

PARTRIDGE: I'd not mind smashing a window. Or something. No, something better than that. Would you?

NEWBOLD: Yes.

PARTRIDGE: You do get strung up here. In this place. Don't you.

NEWBOLD: Yes.

PARTRIDGE: But—well—Oh, well, it's no good trying to change it.

NEWBOLD: No.

PARTRIDGE: You and old Heffer don't hit it off, do you?

NEWBOLD: No. I don't hit it off at all. What do you think would have happened if I'd been in Macready's?

PARTRIDGE: Macready's? Oh, nothing special. Nothing different. Oh—worse.

NEWBOLD: Yes. Worse. . . .

PARTRIDGE: Can't change it.

NEWBOLD: No.

PARTRIDGE: I'd—I'd lie to anyone, oh anyone here. I suppose I've got more drive. *I* should be in Macready's.

NEWBOLD: Yes.

PARTRIDGE: This isn't much. . . . But what's so good about home? I must get a new watch strap—next time.
(*They walk up the high street. Early-closing day.*)

68. INT. DAY

Common room.

PREFECT: Newbold!

(NEWBOLD *looks eagerly.* PREFECT *has a letter.* NEWBOLD *takes it. It is marked O.H.M.S. Inland Revenue.*)

69. INT. DAY

Classroom. NEWBOLD *is seated at desk. Master is speaking.*

NEWBOLD (*V.O.*): Can I afford my own school fees? Well? Now—Where's little Partridge? I miss him. He's very

40

clever. So's she. They both are.

70. INT. DAY

HEFFER'S *study.* HEFFER *reclines as* NEWBOLD *waits.*

HEFFER: You sound supplicant, from what I hear. A T. S. Eliotish sort of word, but you may grasp my meaning. Never mind if you don't. You're not—repeat not—not doing us any good here at Grant's. . . . Are you?

NEWBOLD: No. . . . I think—not.

HEFFER: Well, that at least is something. You're an odd bird, Newbold. In your very ordinary way, of course.

NEWBOLD: Yes.

HEFFER: What do you suggest?

NEWBOLD: I don't know.

HEFFER: You don't know. No. I expect you would like to be in Macready's. Yes?

NEWBOLD: I——

HEFFER: You don't know. Nor do I. What am I to do with you? No, even you can't say you don't know.
(*Pause.*)
You're not up to Macready's are you?

NEWBOLD: No.

HEFFER: You're not up to Grant's are you?

NEWBOLD: No. No. I'm not up to Grant's.

HEFFER: Well. Well, I'm glad to hear it from your own lips, Newbold. Mustn't be too keen. . . . Don't—repeat, don't—be caught snogging. But with you, with you, Newbold, however much you try, it will, I'm afraid, it will make little, no, it will make no difference at all. You may go. I do think it's best. Don't you?
(NEWBOLD *nods and goes.*)

71. EXT. DAY

Bicycle shed. NEWBOLD *looks at his punctured tyre. A junior approaches him.*

JUNIOR: Do it for you?

NEWBOLD: Would you? Oh! Really?

41

JUNIOR: Five—six bob.
NEWBOLD: Oh—O.K.
　　(PARTRIDGE *appears.*)
PARTRIDGE: Two bob would have done it.
NEWBOLD: Yes. I know. I was—tired.

72. EXT. DAY

Swimming-pool. NEWBOLD *watches his wife doing a brilliant crawl,*
beating all around her. HEFFER *is also watching. He turns to* NEW-
BOLD *as the girl's fingers touch the end of the pool in triumph.*
HEFFER: Macready's again, Newbold. There! Macready's!

73. EXT. DAY

Farmyard. School. NEWBOLD *is feeding the pigs with* PARTRIDGE.
NEWBOLD: Fag?
PARTRIDGE: O.K.

74. INT. DAY

Apple loft.
NEWBOLD: I get so hungry.
PARTRIDGE: Yes.
NEWBOLD: I suppose one should lay on parcels.
PARTRIDGE: Sure.
NEWBOLD: Fry-up in your rooms?
PARTRIDGE: That's it.
NEWBOLD: What's your first name?
PARTRIDGE: Ned. I told you.
NEWBOLD: Yes. I do miss her.
PARTRIDGE: Smoking's all right. But not up to much. Not
　　really.
NEWBOLD: No. No. You're right. Not really. All right, then—
　　give it back. . . .
PARTRIDGE: What for?
　　(*He smokes the cigarette.*)

75. INT. DAY

Chapel. Hymn-singing. NEWBOLD *is watching everything intently, including his wife.*

NEWBOLD (*V.O.*): Why's the Head always late? Why is *she* never late? You can't get away from it. . . . It helps you late in life. . . . You must understand the rules . . . *anyone*, anyone can understand them. It's a democratic system, that's the whole point. You've not been singled out because you're special, Newbold, you are not, that's very clear.

76. EXT. DAY
River. NEWBOLD *sculling badly.*

77. INT. DAY
Chapel. Singing.
NEWBOLD (*V.O.*): Endless plunging of the bog. The piano. Playing.

78. INT. DAY
Music room. Boy playing.

79. EXT. DAY
School grounds. NEWBOLD *walking alone.*
NEWBOLD (*V.O.*): What's going to happen to the place? To any of us. Oh God—the endless bloody goodness of the *Observer*. Partridge is quite right. He's quite right.

80. EXT. DAY
Playing fields. NEWBOLD *and* PARTRIDGE. *They look at the country-side.*
PARTRIDGE: Oh, God—God, send us a motorway. Send us a motorway and an airport.

81. EXT. DAY
Countryside. NEWBOLD *and* PARTRIDGE *look around them. A tweedy woman in distance.*
PARTRIDGE: I wonder if old Tester's wife is on the Pill.
NEWBOLD: What a phrase. Who cares—about her—or it.

43

PARTRIDGE: *She* should.

NEWBOLD: Yes. I suppose—I suppose she should. Keep them occupied—like us.

PARTRIDGE: What?

NEWBOLD: Oh—nothing. I'm getting spots.

PARTRIDGE: So I noticed.

(*They walk on in silence.*)

82. EXT. DAY

Countryside. PARTRIDGE *and* NEWBOLD.

PARTRIDGE: There's not much local talent is there

NEWBOLD: No. No, there isn't.

PARTRIDGE: You and me of course.

NEWBOLD: Well—you. . . .

(*They walk on.*)

83. EXT. DAY

School. PARTRIDGE *and* NEWBOLD. *Enter from walk.* NEWBOLD'S *wife is playing tennis.*

PARTRIDGE: God!

NEWBOLD: What?

PARTRIDGE: What? Oh, nothing. Just—oh. This place is a drag.

(MRS. NEWBOLD *does a hefty service.*)

That was rather good.

NEWBOLD: Yes, I suppose it was.

84. EXT. DAY

Playing fields. NEWBOLD *and his wife.*

NEWBOLD: I don't think I can afford it.

MRS. NEWBOLD: So you keep saying.

NEWBOLD: Well—anyway. . . .

MRS. NEWBOLD: Yes. . . .

NEWBOLD: I shall miss Partridge.

MRS. NEWBOLD: Who? Oh yes—Partridge. You were friendly weren't you?

NEWBOLD: You could always jack out into town . . . for a bird.

MRS. NEWBOLD: Oh, yes?

44

NEWBOLD: Well, that's what he said. Not that, well, I think he
　　did. I say, I *have* missed you. I don't think he *did*.
　　(*Pause.*)

85. EXT. DAY
School grounds. NEWBOLD *and wife.*
NEWBOLD: You look very attractive.
MRS. NEWBOLD: Thank you.
NEWBOLD: I suppose everyone—everyone in Macready's tells
　　you?
MRS. NEWBOLD: Well—sort of.
NEWBOLD: Yes. . . . You've done very well here. Haven't you?
　　I mean haven't you? As well, I mean, perhaps even better,
　　even better than *you* expected? Yes.
MRS. NEWBOLD: Yes. I suppose—so. I shall look back on it——
NEWBOLD: As not—not, what you would call wasted time?
MRS. NEWBOLD: Oh, no. Not wasted. Not wasted time at all.
NEWBOLD: End of term. Just about. Well—almost. May I—hold
　　your hand?
MRS. NEWBOLD: All right. Till we get round the hill. . . . I've
　　got the Debating Society tonight. I'm rather good.
NEWBOLD: I'm sure. . . .
　　(*They walk hand in hand. He watches her. She is distracted.*)
　　End of term. Home. . . .
　　(*She laughs, leaves his hand and runs on.*)

86. INT. DAY
HEFFER'S *study.* HEFFER, *elegant as ever, gazes at* NEWBOLD.
HEFFER: I don't think I ever expected much of you—not really
　　—Newbold. But it's been rather worse than I'd anticipated.
　　What are your own feelings? Do you feel the—the
　　enterprise—was worth it? I don't mean you haven't
　　tried. I know you have but it isn't that at all. Is it? What
　　do you feel?
NEWBOLD: Not—not a success, Heffer. I did try.
HEFFER: Oh, I know. Trying, like patriotism isn't enough
　　though, is it? Not for Grant's. I should, well, I should

45

think it all over during the holidays. About coming back
I mean. There are other places. . . . Other things to do. . . .
But I have to make *this* one work. I can't afford passengers
. . . I just can't. . . . Sorry, Newbold. . . . I won't say "see
you next term . . .". Good luck.
(*He shakes hands.* . . . NEWBOLD *gulps and goes.* HEFFER
stares dreamily out of his window at the playing fields.)

87. INT. DAY
Chapel. TESTER *is addressing the School.*
TESTER: . . . not in any sense partisan, I must say Grant's . . .
Grant's has done well. Well, more than well, and I confess
to you I cannot say why. The why I know not. The
wherefore must be, indeed, I know is—Heffer.

88. INT. DAY
Chapel. C.U. HEFFER.

89. INT. DAY
Chapel.
TESTER: Well—another term, yet another year for some of us.

90. INT. DAY
NEWBOLD'S *room. He is packing.* PARTRIDGE *looks in.*
PARTRIDGE: Packing?
NEWBOLD: That's right.

91. INT. DAY
School hall. Parents, boys, etc. Prize giving. NEWBOLD *watches his
wife going up to receive prize.*

92. INT. DAY
Chapel. Once again NEWBOLD *looks to his wife. She is gazing, wrapt,
at the* HEADMASTER.

93. INT. DAY
Chapel.

TESTER: Again, yes once again, I must congratulate Macready's
—for the efforts—their achievements (sporting *and*—oh
yes *and*, more than—and—academic) and also, also I must
mention Grant's. Grant's. . . . It's Head of House . . . and
—well—end of term. What is to be said? The Chaplain
has spoken. Your Housemasters, the Heads of Houses,
you've all spoken. I think—well, why not, let's end as we
began—I think—we began . . . with A. H. Clough. Whom
you will remember. . . . "Say Not the Struggle Naught
Availeth". . . . School. . . .
(*Everyone rises and sings.* MRS. NEWBOLD *weeps as she sings.*
NEWBOLD *stares ahead of him.* PARTRIDGE *sings well. So
does* HEFFER. *Everyone seems content and relieved—except*
NEWBOLD, *who is still bewildered and his wife who's grieving
in her way.*)

94. EXT. DAY
School grounds. NEWBOLD *looks around him. Alone.* PARTRIDGE
avoids him. He turns into the House for the last time.

95. EXT. DAY
School grounds. Chauffeur is seeing MR. *and* MRS. NEWBOLD *into
their hired car.* NEWBOLD *looks round but no one is in sight.*

96. INT. DAY
Car.
NEWBOLD: Well—they none of them said goodbye.
MRS. NEWBOLD: No. Why should they?
NEWBOLD: Quite. . . . Did you, did you bring your holiday
task?
MRS. NEWBOLD: Yes.
NEWBOLD: *Did* you? Yes. Good old Macready's. . . . Poor old
Grant's. . . . Anyway—good for Crampton. . . . At least, we've
the holidays . . . our little holidays.
MRS. NEWBOLD: What?
NEWBOLD: Nothing. Old Partridge is staying with his step-
mother.

47

MRS. NEWBOLD: You surprise me.

NEWBOLD: I looked for him. To say goodbye. But he seemed to disappear. . . .

97. Ext. Day

School drive. The hired car sweeps past the victorian Gothic and pasture. Both NEWBOLDS *look out of the car windows.*

98. Ext. Day

PARTRIDGE, *a lonely figure against the playing fields watches the car disappear. He takes out a packet of cigarettes and lights one.*

THE END